The Astronomer's Pearl

Poems
by
George Young

George Young

Snake~Nation~Press
Founded 1989
110 West Force Street
Valdosta, Georgia 31601

Snake Nation Press wishes to thank:
Barbara Passmore & The Price-Campbell Foundation
The Georgia Council for the Arts
Gloria & Wilby Coleman
Lowndes/Valdosta Arts Commission
Dean Poling & *The Valdosta Daily Times*
Blake Ellis
Our Subscribers

Snake Nation Press, the only independent literary press in south Georgia, publishes two *Snake Nation Reviews,* a book of poetry by a single author each year, and a book of fiction by a single author each year. Unsolicited submissions of fiction, essays, art, and poetry are welcome throughout the year but will not be returned unless a stamped, self-addressed envelope is included. We encourage simultaneous submissions.

Subscriptions
Individuals $30
Institutions $40
Foreign $40
Sample Copy $12 (includes shipping)

Published by Snake Nation Press
110 West Force Street
Valdosta, Georgia 31601

Printed and bound in the United States of America.

Copyright © George Young 2013
All Rights Reserved

The poems in this book are works of fiction. Names, characters, places and incidents are either products of the author's imagination or are used fictitiously. Any resemblance to actual persons, living or dead, is entirely coincidental.

No part of this book may be reproduced in any form, except for the quotation of brief passages, or for non-profit educational use, without prior written permission from the copyright holder.

ISBN: 978-0-9883029-0-7

The Astronomer's Pearl

Poems
by
George Young

Snake~Nation~Press
Founded 1989
110 West Force Street
Valdosta, Georgia 31601
www.snakenationpress.org

Artist's Statement

   Two of the *ah-ha* moments of my life occurred when I was growing up.

   One was when I read a book, *The Cry and the Covenant*, which is about the tragic life of Ignaz Semmelweis who discovered that fatal child-bed fever in women, called puerperal sepsis, could be prevented if physicians simply washed their hands before a delivery (although no one at the time would believe him). I was so impressed with this story, I decided then and there that I wanted to be a doctor.

   The other one happened in the back seat of a car one summer on a trip to Alaska with my parents when I read Keat's amazing "Ode to Melancholy" in an old poetry anthology I had picked out from my grandmother's bookcase in Seattle, and I immediately began trying to write (poorly) poems of my own.

   But the years of studying medicine made it difficult for me to write poetry until I was well into my practice. Then, finding I needed something more in my life than just science, and like one of my heros, William Carlos Williams, I began writing. And as you will see from the poems in this book, I believe that a good poem, like a good diagnosis, should be sharp and clear, not wooly and hard to understand.

   The idea that science and art are two separate realms is, for me, a myth. Scientists can love poetry and poets can love science. Murray Gel-Mann, the famous physicist, in his book, *Quark and Jaguar*, summed it up best when he said, "The beauty of nature is manifested just as much in the elegance of the fundamental principles of science as in the cry of a loon or the trails of bioluminescence made by porpoises at night." *Amen.*

- George Young

Dedication

This book is dedicated to my daughter, Shelby.

I would also like to thank my wife Peg for her loving support, and many thanks to Jean Arambula, Roberta George and my son Greg, for their thoughtful assistance with the manuscript.

About the Cover

The cover photo was taken by my wife Peg while we were on a recent trip to Ireland in May, 2012. We liked it so much that she has it framed and it is hanging on our wall with the title: "Heading Home." I thought it fit with several of the poems in the book having to do with growing old, especially the one: "Sonnet For Two Old Dogs." Are the man and the dog heading for the house in the background, or perhaps for a place unseen around the bend, or for the mountain or even for somewhere beyond?

Contents

One
Big Bang   12
Ice And Fire   13
The Terrible Sweetness Of Being   15
The Face Of Evil   16
My Father's Hands   18
The Ladybug   19
To My Son   20
The Wound Dresser   21
The Immense Heartlessness Of The Universe   23
The Blossoming   24
Flowers In The Yucatan   25
The Secret Of Life   27
Notes From Inside A Water Lily   28
Conversation With A Great Blue Heron   29
Nietzsche's Horse   30
Fin de Siecle   32

Two
The Invitation   34
The Bird Of Paradise   35
Emerson's Aphasia   36
Fear And Trembling   37
The Ornithologist's Confession   38
Recompense At Noon   39
Sonnet For Two Old Dogs   40
The Beetle And The Butterfly   41
Proof Of The Soul   42
The Red Bulls   43
The Sweetness Of Disordered Air   45
The Cremation Of Frida Kahlo   46
Black Night   47
Darwin   48
Age   49
Out There   50
Truckstop   51
Shooting Stars   52
The Continuum   53
Sonnet On My Kinship With The Hymenoptera   54
Birdskin   55
A Tale Of Two Universes   57
Hutala, Afghanistan   58

Three
The Homecoming   60
The Secrets Of Glass   61
Mt. Katahdin   62
Audubon   64
To A Blue-throated Hummingbird   66
His Eyes   67
The Sparks Of Creation   69
Sunday Morning   71
Good Dog   72
O Savage Spirit   73
Bartolomé de las Casas   74
Note To Myself   76
Nature Trail, Saguaro National Park   77
Deep Time   78
Garden Of The Lost   79
Judgment Day   81

Acknowledgments

American Poets and Poetry: "His Eyes" (under the title: "God's Eye")
The Annals Of Internal Medicine: "The Blossoming"; "The Face Of Evil" (also appearing in the book: *Primary Care, more poems by physicians*)
The Aurorean: "Deep Time"; "The Lady Bug"; "Truckstop"; "The Terrible Sweetness Of Being" (chosen as "Best Poem of the Issue" and nominated for a Pushcart Prize) and also appearing in the anthology, *Favorites From the First Fifteen Years*, published by Encircle Publications.
Avocet: "The Continuum"; "Sunday Morning"
The Cape Rock: "Garden Of The Lost"; "Big Bang"; "Ice And Fire" (also nominated for a Pushcart Prize)
The Comstock Review: "Notes From Inside A Water Lily"
Diner: "Emerson's Aphasia" (also appearing in the book: *Primary Care, more poems by physicians*)
Edgz: "Recompense At Noon"
Epicenter: "Fin de Siecle" (under the title: "A Letter To Thomas Hardy"); "Proof Of The Soul"
Georgetown Review: "Black Night"
The Iconoclast: "Good Dog"
Journal of the American Medical Association: "Judgment Day"; "The Wound Dresser"
The Literary Review: "Conversation With A Great Blue Heron"; "The Secret Of Life"
Mobius: "The Sparks Of Creation"; "Shooting Stars"
Orange Willow Review: "Flowers In The Yucatan"
Pearl: "The Homecoming"
Peregrine: "The Immense Heartlessness Of The Universe"
Pharos: "Nietzsche's Horse"; "The Cremation Of Frida Kahlo"
Plainsongs: "Bartolome de las Cases"; "Birdskin"; "My Father's Hands" (an award winning poem of that issue); "Sonnet For Two Old Dogs"
Poet & Critic: "Oh Savage Spirit"
Poet Lore: "Darwin"; "The Invitation"; "Out There"; "The Red Bulls"

Potato Eyes: "The Secrets Of Glass"
Primary Care, more poems by physicians: "Hutala Afghanistan"
Sou'wester: "Mt. Katahdin"
Tiger's Eye: "The Ornithologist's Confession"; "To My Son"
360 Degrees: "The Sweetness Of Disordered Air" (also appearing in the book, *Cabin Fever, Poets at Joaquin Miller's Cabin*)
Westview: "Nature Trail, Saguaro National Monument"; "Note To Myself"
White Heron: "To A Blue-throated Hummingbird" (also appearing in *Bear Deluxe*)
Willard & Maple: "A Tale Of Two Universes" (under the title: "The Mind's Sky")
Willow Review: "Audubon"; "Fear And Trembling"
Wisconsin Review: "Age"
Yarrow, A Journal Of Poetry: "The Beetle And The Butterfly"; "The Bird Of Paradise" (under the title, "God's Bird"). "The Beetle And The Butterfly" also appeared in the book: *Winners, a Retrospective of the Washington Prize*

One

*World is suddener than we fancy it.
...crazier... than we think,
incorrigibly plural. I peel and portion
a tangerine and spit the pips and feel
the drunkenness of things being various.*
            Louis MacNeice
                (from his poem "Snow.")

Big Bang
>   *(for Neil de Grasse Tyson)*

The astronomer's pearl,
held up between his forefinger and thumb, the color of
a cloudy sun,
>   "This," he says,
"is the original size of the universe."

You reel—

(100 billion galaxies, 100 billion stars in ours,
our blue and white marble
circling in the void, the coruscating lights of New York City,
the Grand
Canyon, dandelions, the pupil
of the human eye,
the tiny
quiver at the mouth)—as he places it all

in the palm of your mind.

Ice and Fire
> *Paul Klee contracted progressive systemic sclerosis (scleroderma) in 1935.*

A man is slowly turning into an ice bird,
into a hard glossy thing
with a beak.
                He sits in a wheelchair
in the winter coldlight of a sanitarium, his claws
gripping a brush,
                painting the picture of his own death.

Switzerland, 1940.

Back in Germany,
before he became a bird, he painted a bird, delicate
and blue, in the "Twittering Machine."

Now his brush strokes are thick,
his colors somber.
                He doesn't see himself
as a bird, but as a stick man.

As he paints,
the tips of his fingers are turning white, aching
as if dipped in ice water.
                His skin, his
joints, the very scaffolding of his lungs are freezing.

So
he paints the background
of his "Death and Fire" in deep shades
of red and orange—
                at the center, a gleaming white skull

with the word "Tod" (death in German)
forming its features—
        a stick man approaching bravely
to stab the skull with a stake—
        and above it all,
shining on the misshapen skull, shining
on the stick man too,
        the hot yellow globe of sun.

The Terrible Sweetness Of Being

Here comes that careless boy with his stick,
sauntering
through the field below my window, whacking
the heads off flowers—
like an idle God.
Stevens says:
Death is the mother of beauty.
Yes.
Tree harps in the wind.
Whack.
O silken remains.
Whack.
And the air is lilac-scented.
Lilac.

The Face Of Evil

Perhaps it was the howls
from the kennels, or the merciless insomnia
that grips men of thought, but that night Louis Pasteur
had a frightful dream that his little patient, Joseph Meister, was
dying.

He knew the symptoms, having witnessed them himself
as a boy in Arbois.

The snapping jaws, foam-flecked, the slobbering bite.
Then the clumsy attempt at treatment,
cauterization at the smithy with a red-hot iron, screams,
the smell of burning flesh.
And inevitably, later, the faint tingling in the cicatrix,
the suffocation at the very sight of water,
the paralysis, the coma and death, always the death.

He woke to the wind scratching at the window like a dog.

But had he not been careful?... trephining the skulls
of dogs, inoculating infected tissue under their scarlet brain-caps;
the transfer to rabbits, their spinal cords
hanging in flasks, shriveling, like tiny criminals on the gallows;
then turning the evil
back on itself by injecting it into infected dogs... who lived!

Light came, that lion, to the grounds of Villeneuve l'Etang.

And that day, July 6, 1885, Joseph, age nine, hands, legs, thighs
purple with bites from a rabid dog,
would become the first to receive the injections
of the rabbit spinal cord into the skin of his abdomen,

crying at first, then
submitting quietly under the watchful eyes
of "dear Monsieur Pasteur."

What do we do in the face of evil?
Consider the exact arc that curved from Arbois
to Paris.

And consider this...
fifty-five years later, on June 14, 1940, a sad day
for the "City of Light,"
the knock of a rifle-butt on a gate, and the gatekeeper
who would commit suicide to avoid opening Pasteur's burial crypt
to the Nazis.
That gatekeeper's name was Joseph Meister.

My Father's Hands

crossed over his chest as he slept, rising
and falling with each breath—

I remember
the hard artery ticking
at the wrist, bulging veins as blue as smoke, bones
on the back
standing out like a bird's foot, flesh
between bones as sunken as four little graves,
the thin skin
as intricate as a Turkish carpet, a brown design,
the map of a life spent out in the sun.

I remember when I was a child how the hands wrote
that tiny quick script,
conspired expertly with a hammer and nail,
fired a handgun,
tied on the tiniest fly,
caught my fastest fastball.

And I remember
how they lay in the coffin—waxen, perfect, still.

Now they are writing this.

The Lady Bug

Spring in Taos. Dazzling snow on the mountain. Gold sunlight in the plaza. A brand-new Rolls Royce convertible, red, shiny, parked at the curb in front of a restaurant. People walk by and whistle. Across the street the girls in the art gallery watch to see who will come out of the restaurant and hop in. Beside the restaurant a dilapidated shack with green grass and weeds in the front yard, a broken-down fence along the sidewalk, the vertical slats of the fence painted green, weathered, some askew, some falling down. Forgive me, God-of-all-things, if I stop and stare, not at the Rolls Royce, but at the peeling green paint, the grain of the wood of the fence; at a lady bug, bright orange with black spots, crawling slowly across a board.

To My Son

You, small flower open, grain of sand
on the beach, one beautiful grain—

don't try to undo all the folded lies.
Half-close your eyes and marvel

at the flickering world, the pebbles of light,
the violet mountains, the jeweled spider

web, the striped snake swimming across
the lake. Pick one red cherry

and crush it between your teeth.
Don't try to analyze the sky. Even its

stars are bound to die.
Remember, your piano, all its ivory and black

keys, its wires and soft hammers, its polished
wood, is *not* the music, *you are!*

And finally, imagine a mystery
that feels compassion for your fate. It helps.

The Wound Dresser

> *...not one do I miss,*
> *An attendant follows holding a tray,*
> *he carries a refuse pail,*
> *Soon to be filled with clotted rags and blood...*
> From *Leaves Of Grass*

Flying back from Richmond
I invited Walt to come along. He took
the window seat.

We talked
Civil War, about what I'd seen: half-filled ditches
and worn-down, grassy parapets;

photographs of young men
lying in rows, backs arched, mouths open,
as if some rapture had taken them;

long knives and surgical saws
and little steel instruments in glass cases.
He told me of arms and legs

piled high behind tents;
of white skeletons unburied in the leaves;
of that distant sound, like tearing

paper, a thousand rifled
muskets, what killed so many men.
Then he looked out the window

at America, 30,000 feet below,
the green squares, the silver serpentine ribbons.

I've seen it all before you know, he said,
In my mind, this land, our land,
from Virginia to California. I dressed its wounds.
I grieved its flag-draped coffins,

I sang its songs, the very songs you see
in that book on your lap. I leaned back and closed
my eyes. When I awoke he was gone.

The Immense Heartlessness Of The Universe

Amelia to Howland: *Come in.*
Radio out!
(What's the chance a single speck of dust in the sky
will land on the back of your hand
in Kansas?)
Come in. Come in.

And an invisible angel, deaf,
blind, in pain,
sits in her wheelchair all day and grieves, never
to reach out, to wrap her arms around
her lost love again.

And what Scott found at the south pole: the absence of
imagination, corrosive cold,
whiteness, whiteness, whiteness, the mask
we cannot see behind.

And in the snowy dawn
crows land like mortar rounds
on the white lawn
of the "City of Hope." Then as the mother of a stricken child
watches from the window—
they surge into flight like black smoke.

The Blossoming

Genevieve
in my office, ancient, her fat chart in my hands....
psoriasis, arthritis, Crohn's disease, two husbands (long gone)
and now
small cell carcinoma of the lung.

"How
was the chemo?" I ask.

She has on red
high-heels, a full white dress,
a green silk scarf tied carefully around her neck,
just a hint
of perfume, and on her head
a huge straw hat with a scarlet feather....

to hide her baldness.

Everything
becomes clearer when I stand beside
this one flower.

Flowers In The Yucatan

Here, as an old man
                walking my way to heaven
down a dusty limestone road that redoubles the sun's heat,
                                            it's time
to begin to relearn my soul,
                it's time to begin to understand how
the unblinking eye
                of an iguana on a rock can illuminate
                                  the world.

Turning onto a trail into the jungle, I feel my face
beginning to slip off my skull.
                      Soon, I will be a dancing skeleton.

What I'm really looking for
is flowers, red flowers, to trample on
                            before I die.
What I find is a pile of cut stones
and an *aguada*, a pool of brackish water surrounded by trees,
and at its edge, like white hands in a dark robe,
                                  two flowering orchids.

So I sit all afternoon
on a rock, listening to the Blue-crowned Motmots,
reading the *Popol Vuh,*
                      thinking about the Maya and their fabulous
God, Kukulcan, the feathered serpent who rose
                                as the evening star,

trying to imagine
this lurid flower of another mind, until
                          the sun bloodies the west
and the God himself rises,
                gold in the blue shell of the sky.

The Secret Of Life

Even as the murderous gardener
kneels in the grass and drives his screwdriver

deep into the milk heart of a last renegade
growing on the front lawn,

the sly dandelions
with their gauzy globes on slender red tubes

are poised like bombs
in the weedlot behind the nursing home

where the skinny old lady with Einstein hair
is leaning out of her wheelchair

to pour water from a paper cup
on the red pansies she is planting; and

just as the swaying sleeve
of her moldy sweater detonates a row

of the puffballs, a gust of wind swirls down
and hurls a hundred tiny messengers

aloft on their journey to the stratosphere,
Madagascar, who knows where.

Notes From Inside A Water Lily

Morning in its new frock coat
takes strychnine and tea on the bank. Noon comes
gorgeous. And the plagiarist moon in the blue.

We rock, you and I—sparks at the center of gleam, floating
on the emerald scum, among silt and weeds,
rinsed by the calming wind—

the sybaritic eyes
of one of the opaline faces in the lake.
I write this all down with a languorous laugh.

We are seeking alertness, the spiritual,
find tumble and shine.
Each moment melts silver. You and I, our little weather.

We are slick-eyed with the dazzling flakes
of air, water, like cut tinfoil.
Twilight on the lake, a violet mirror, a dream—

you trail your hand in the flame. Then
pitched in the lily of night,
in the mouth of a star, we are light-pierced, divine.

Conversation With A Great Blue Heron

"I came out to the pond to ask you a question," I say.
"What shall I do with my life?"

You are studying a shadow in the water.

A single-engined airplane clatters up
from the city airport, towing a white glider into the sky.

You spear.

"Last night on the stairs
for the first time I felt the death of promise," I say.

The fish you just caught is now a bulge in your neck.

"And I don't care about
the box scores in the morning papers anymore."

You raise one foot and freeze, a drop of water glistening
from your toe. I watch your yellow eye.

"Catch a fish," you say.

Nietzsche's Horse

What are we to make of it—
syphilitic spirochetes
spinning in his brain, creating some wild delusion,
or a moment of clarity?

Turin, Italy, 1889. Cold, brilliant day.

And Nietzsche,
bushy-haired, deep eye-wells red, with a huge mustache,
walking through the Piazza Carlo Alberto, hears
hoof beats on the cobblestones,
sees an old horse, eyes wide, head thrown back,
being whipped by a coachman,

and runs,
throwing his arms around the arched neck of the horse
(like a new moon embracing the old)
and, weeping, whispers something in its ear.

There are birds of light in the air

and irony:
this Greek scholar, this most arrogant of men whose credo
is the *will to power*,
who has preached that sympathy is weakness—
saves a horse.

Then he collapses,
and they carry him back to his room
(the beginning of eleven more years of a life of insanity).
Was it madness—
or perhaps something else, more human,

which even he could not hide:
the gift of the fire of comprehension (stolen for us from the gods
by Prometheus)
for which we pay by enduring the pain of all horses?

That day the distant Alps burning like white candles.

Fin de Siecle
(To Thomas Hardy)

A hundred years ago today you wrote of your *darkling thrush*
singing of blessed hope in the desolation of a winter, that winter
for you the *crypt of your century's corpse.* And for us now too,
the same desolation. I think of Eliot's *hollow men...leaning together;*
of Auden in his dive on *Fifty-Second Street*; of Wiesel watching
a child being hung by the Gestapo, someone asking, *where is God
now*? and Wiesel thinking, *He is hanging here on the gallows*;
of the perfect outline of a human body etched on the sidewalk
in downtown Hiroshima; of Kurtz in Cambodia describing a diamond
bullet hitting him between the eyes when he realized the genius
of the enemy: hacking off the vaccinated arms of their own children.
And I think of you today because I'm sitting in my garden listening
to a mourning dove cooing, wondering about the language of birds.
How human of you to think birds sing because their hearts are
bursting with hope. I'm afraid they sing for more mundane reasons.
But I'm glad to report we do still believe in Dickinson's *thing
with feathers*, and the dove is cooing—cool so cool, not mourning.

Two

Oh burning world....
Baying dog in the valley, train rolling far away,
....you turn out to be my sweetest dream and illusion.

Hermann Hesse

The Invitation
     (after Rilke)

You don't have to be special to feel it.
Take a walk in the woods, alone.
Look, listen, step softly.

You will feel a *click* as if
a key, fitting perfectly, turned in an oiled lock.
And a door opens.

Step out, step into the same place your
ancestors stepped into—
this quick world, the beginning.

You are matter contemplating itself.
Search for signs—
the green expanse, gaudy in the straw-gold sun;

the amethyst dew, shy drops about to vanish;
split trunk; falling leaf; lambent stones;
the red reward of a bird.

You are here
and everything here is waiting for you,
a flower opening only once.

The Bird Of Paradise
(from notes found in Linnaeus's desk after His death, 1778)

This rare avian species is footless
but unimaginably beautiful:

its head a satiny yellow,
throat a patch of iridescent green,
breast, back and wings russet...
and emerging from under its wings, long plumes
fanning out behind like streamers from the sun.

The Dutch explorer, Van Linschoten,
has made extravagant claims:

that having no feet this bird cannot roost
so lives only in the ether of heaven,
perpetually on the wing...

it drinks directly from the clouds,
catches high blown insects from the air...

and the only time it ever comes to earth
is when it dies, then its body falls
and is sometimes found by natives on the jungle floor
of an island called Aru.

We have seen the skin of one here in Sweden,
badly mangled, at the museum in Uppsala,
and would pay dearly to see more.
The devout sometimes kneel and pray to it.

I have assigned it the Latin name, *Paradisea apoda*.

Emerson's Aphasia
*"Nature...disdains words...yet solicits
the pure in heart to draw on all its omnipotence."
(from his essay, "Fate")*

In the carriage down from Concord, 1879—

one wheel bounces over a pothole
and a skeletal hand reaches out to grip the open window.

Then a distant thunder-clap
as the gold flood of sunlight shuts off.

"The- the- the- How do you call what stores up water
till it suddenly- suddenly- what shall I say?
Not squeezed out."

"A sponge," the other passenger suggests.

"No, no," with the sweetest of smiles and a sweeping
motion of his other hand up to the sky.

"The clouds perhaps?" is the next suggestion.

"Yes, the clouds are rolling up."

The carriage lurches and it starts to rain, the drops like bites
of a tiny kitten on the back of his hand.

"Shall I close the window?" the passenger asks.

"No," comes the answer. "No, no, no!"

Fear And Trembling

is you on a winter night, alone
on a concrete bench,

overlooking the ghost of a frozen lake,
bombarded

by starlight that started out
long before you were born.

The Ornithologist's Confession
(for G.M.H.)

Can birds be a religion?

                    O Vermilion Flycatcher, O Living

Fire—

this morning the forest is coruscating with eleven

kinds of green, and I'm climbing

into its raucous mist

                    looking for you—

my *Chevalier*.

I have a mystical itch.

Recompense At Noon

You know
ecstasy is bogus
(guitar riff, sunset, love-making, sweet wine)

and dread clouds are out there, always,
the low horizon proceeding closer,
God unknowable,

but still—
              this light

scattering green diamonds in the grass,
plumping the grapes—
                          this feeling

of just walking on the earth under the lavish sun
like a candle

melting under the flame.

Sonnet For Two Old Dogs

I'm walking Abby, my ancient golden retriever,
down Old St. Vrain Road,
pomegranate cliffs on the left, crashing
stream on the right, mortality
dogging my heels like a shadow.
Must even the best wine glass eventually break?
Do all flowers have to crumple?
The skyline mountain arches its back like a cat, as four
silver pigeons veer near the cliffs.
And when it comes
will it be a red burst in the skull,
or slick as a seal entering the water?
I stop, the sun a gold tooth in the clouds.
It must be against the law to stand here so happy.

The Beetle and the Butterfly

The evolution of the idea of
evolution
proceeded much like evolution does itself sometimes,
simultaneously, in the lush
jungles of two minds. One slow as an ebony
beetle crawling through the grass. The other swift
as a fragile blue butterfly glittering across
a splash of sunlight.

Darwin, standing at the London Zoo in 1838,
staring out from under his beetling brows into the eyes
of Jenny, the ape, knew it before
anyone else.
Those eyes stared back! But with his
beetling ways he could not bring himself to publish...

until (at last)
in 1858, when young Wallace
on his cot, febrile with malaria, in the Malay archipelago,
remembering what he had read in Malthus,
suddenly had two iridescent wings dance through his head
and penned
his feverish letter to Darwin.

The rest
you know. Survival of the fittest idea. God
cast out of Eden by man. All that.

Proof Of The Soul
                (April 10, 1910)

"The ether-self floating out at the time of death
   must weigh something." So said Dr. MacDougall

as he carefully arranged his Fairbanks Imperial
   Grocer's Scale under the bed of his dying patient

(tuberculosis, poor man, his lungs laboring stertorously).
   And at the exact moment of death the end beam

dropped and remained there as if a weight had been
   lifted off the bed. Later, it took the weight of two

silver dollars to lift the beam back to balance.
   Interestingly, when the same thing was done with

a dying dog, there was no weight loss at all. Since then
   no one has ventured to repeat these experiments.

The Red Bulls

Sometimes the glittering thread called time
        loops back on itself;
    in an instant
           the present touches the past.

So, at Altamira, Spain, in 1879,
      in a newly discovered cave,
Don Marcelino's five-year old daughter, Maria,
        shrieks
as he lifts a trembling candle flame and they see
         the enormous eye of a bison
      staring back at them,
then, a whole bestiary on the cave walls:
      bison, wild boars, horses; in ocher,
          gold and dun;
        as if painted yesterday.

When Maria reaches out and touches the red bull,
     the color
         comes off on her finger.

Of course no one would believe Don Marcelino.
     Denounced by the famous prehistorian, Cartailhac,
  for concocting a hoax,
      he died.
    The cave was sealed for 23 years.

But finally,
     Cartailhac came to see for himself.
   The cave was unsealed.
        What he said when he entered is not recorded.

  We know he immediately asked Maria to take him
to Don Marcelino's grave
    where he took off his hat and apologized.
  He realized
 the significance of these ancient pictures.

For here, at Altamira, during the ice age,
     human artists created
 the invisible universe of dreams
  smoldering behind the eyes
   of the hunters squatting around their campfires,
 a universe haunted by
     spirit animals.

And little Maria
  that first night, in 1879, after her great discovery,
    went to sleep
  to the sound of hooves
     clattering in the dark.

The Sweetness Of Disordered Air
(Wyoming, there is nothing out there except clouds)

Driving north to Sheridan, you and I, the sky
just shy of crushing us,

we gradually become aware
that Plato must have been wrong.

For there are violet bruises, pearly bosses, dark hugs
and streamers of white silk. But how

could there ever be
a single template for a cloud?

Mist shapes itself in the empty sky
without a plan. Clouds

are born, clouds hurry, clouds die. It seems God
does play dice with the universe.

When the rain starts
squirming on the wind-shield, you peel an orange.

I pop a wedge in my mouth, open the window
to spit out a pip, and suddenly

we are splashed
by the delicious wet air of Wyoming.

The Cremation Of Frida Kahlo

After the flesh was gone
they say her bones burned violet
before they crumbled.

Toad-eyed Diego wept
and warned the world, "She'll clump into your heart
and then she'll eat it. She ate mine."

And on the heap of white ash that had been her
a steel rod of spine glowed red.

Black Night

Right now
a penguin stands in Antarctica,
its head drooping in the black night,
an egg between its legs—

and a Mayan God, tipped
on its side,
stares with blank eyes
at a pool in the forest covered with leaves—

and you
sit in an airport,
flight delayed, clutching your bag, far, far
from those you love.

Darwin

The kindly gentleman from Down,
during the last ice-age of his *Origin of Species*, mammoths freezing
    in the bogs,
diverted himself mornings strolling the Sandwalk in his woods.
And once, as he stood still, musing,
gall fly larva devouring their own mothers, two baby squirrels
    scampered
up his legs and across his back, mistaking him for an old tree.
Evenings he played backgammon with Emma,
lions, their mouths fitting perfectly the throats of zebras, killing
    and gorging.
For supper he liked bread and soup.

Age

Carry
is subtraction,
a coin
a game of pick-up
in your pocket.
sticks.
Take it out
In the end
from time to time
what's left
and flip it.
of spring's
On one side it says:
great green
you are alive.
gold manifoldness
On the other:
is this:
you are going to die.
winter's
When you read it
brave straws
shout: but!
spearing
and turn it over.
the snow.

Out There

Twist off a bit and eat it.

Hook it, feel it tugging on your line, too deep to see,
    swimming below in the dark water.

Plunge your arm through the tumbling waterfall to feel it.

Even stain it with your colors: peacock's tail, the blue eyes,
    the slabs of bloody meat—

but it all turns out to be tempered, tampered with,
    shifted, shuffled, recast, *unknowable*—

and, though you sense it is out there, from its size
    and shape and weight,

it slips away like silk catching on your rough hands.

Truckstop
    (after Edward Hopper)

Outside, trucks and cars Doppler by in the night
and an American flag

cracks in the wind, pole chain clanging.
In here, a man with a beard

works on a crossword.
From a wavy poster on the wall a beautiful girl

offers me a plate of ham and eggs,
her huge enamel smile fake as the dusty bouquet

of plastic roses on my table.
A mother with two kids is trying to cut a hamburger

in half with a plastic knife.
A waitress hurries over with my refill.

No one talks. The linoleum floor needs
mopping. The lights

are too bright. Yes. But something else
in here too, almost sublime,

as I pour cream
in my coffee, watch it swirl, raise my cup.

Shooting Stars

On the trail to "Bird Woman Falls"
in Glacier Park, I come upon
a patch of Shooting Stars: tiny flaming purple darts
all pointing down
toward the center of the Earth.

In Basho's famous *haiku*, he looked
carefully and saw a *nazuna* blooming by the hedge!
That's all. He just saw it!
The bones of Zen.

But what Basho couldn't know
in the 17th century,
is that one hundred million years ago flowers
actually changed the world.
Without that soundless explosion of color, without all
the seeds and fruit and grasses
there would be no bees, no birds, no bison. And no us.

There are two minds, East and West.
And there were other minds.

In the New York Museum of Natural History
there's a diorama of Neanderthals
huddled about an open grave, the body
of their dead covered with hundreds of blooming flowers.

Are flowers the answer to nothingness?

Standing quite still on the trail, I look
carefully at the Shooting Stars. I reach out my hand
and touch one gently.

The Continuum

Did you know mountains flow? Heraclitis knew

(and we,
so briefly here,
too)

that stones in the river are becoming water

and the soul is a breath
passed on from father to son.

Sonnet On My Kinship With The Hymenoptera

Climbing west out of Denver (window seat)
reading the life of Michel de Montaigne,
I look down and see my own town: tiny cars
with tiny drivers,
tiny tennis courts, my own house!
And suddenly my mighty self with all its *sturm und drang*
is reduced to something insect-sized.
And I realize (.45 caliber bullet
between the eyes) Montaigne was right:
*"how silly of us to think
that armed with reason we are the lords and masters of
the universe."* Looking down from the airplane now
I am a wasp, buzzing at
my tiny window on the world.

Birdskin
> *"...when the last individual of a race of living*
> *beings breathes no more, another heaven and another*
> *earth must pass before such a one can be again."*
> William Beebe

A rag-doll bird now,
      neck on a string.
           A clean slit up from the cloaca.
The gleaming jewels: the heart, liver, lungs drop
on a newspaper. Pry out the eyes,
      scoop out the skull, the pecan-sized brain
        is delivered with its star-maps.

Nebraska, April, 1887.
  A twelve-year old boy watches an undulating
    banner in the sky,
a quarter of a mile long and one hundred
      yards wide, settle
        across the mudflats,
            a scintillating mirage—birds
      feeding, exhausted,
on their way from Argentina to the Arctic.

The bird's back is brown, its belly buff, its crown
    striped, its bill incredibly long
            and down-curved.
      Its new body
    becomes a stick
        wrapped in cotton, imbedded in the skull.

"Prairie pigeons" they are called.
      Spiraling in on one of their beautiful

revolutions, they offer
a more compact target for the gunners. And
the guileless birds
continue to circle
in spite of the firing, their great numbers
falling.

This is the last bird
        we know about,
      shot in Barbados in 1963 by a hunter
on its lonely flight south,
           its legs are tied together with the thread
of a specimen tag
        that reads "Eskimo Curlew."

The shooting today was "too good."
*   The wagon beds are filled with heaps*
of dead birds,
*   Soon they are dumped on the ground*
*   to rot*
so that more can be taken.

The skin of that last bird
      now rests in a wooden drawer
          in a museum in Philadelphia, its blank eyes
            white
          with wisps of escaping cotton.

A Tale Of Two Universes

Call it astonishment, a gift
of evolution,
but in a far dim time in Africa
a sudden twist in one of our neural networks
led
to an infinite recursion—

as mirrors tilted at the proper angle
will reflect each other endlessly—

this twist
the origin of consciousness,
the Big Bang
in our heads that started an ever-expanding
inner universe.

And look now—

in the early morning dark
Edwin Hubble bends over his desk,
writes of his great discovery: *Light from faint*
galaxies is more red
than light
from bright galaxies
which means they must be flying away—

as the inner subsumes the outer.

Hutala, Afghanistan

A child is not a lion, is not, is not a zero.
Collateral damage can never, never be

excused or written off as just an accident.
The tiny shoes, the braided caps displayed

on the dirt mounds. The grief like a nail
hammered into the skull and no way to pull

it out. Seven boys and two girls and one
young man, about to be married, gone,

gone forever. And the pilot whose rocket
exploded their lives, staring in the dark.

Don't blame God. It's not his fault. Blame
us all. We forgot, children are flowers.

Three

*Where I am, I don't know, I'll never know, in the silence
you don't know, you must go on, I can't go on, I'll go on.*

Samuel Beckett

The Homecoming

We went back.
Thick vines covered the walls
and the gates stood open, though veiled with spider webs.
No flaming sword to repel us.
Inside, the Tree of Life was just a white skeleton.
No birds, no beguiling serpent—they
had long ago been killed off.
My joints ached. Her hair was gray.
We called to Him once, twice, but He did not answer.
The garden was empty.
We stood for awhile holding hands, listening to the dry reeds
clicking in the wind,
then left. A dust storm was coming.

The Secrets Of Glass

The boy Spinoza's
thin, trembling hands are learning
the secrets of Venetian glass, *cristallo*: if you rub
a scratched piece skillfully
it will go a little way back along the road
to its molten state and swallow up its own scratches.

Now in the early Amsterdam evening, the sky
diffused with colors
that have no name, he grinds and polishes painstakingly
in his little room,
working on the ordered parts for a new telescope,
his mind off again in the desert, lost,
perplexed by
those crazy miracles of the old God:
the burning bush, water springing from the rock.

And all the while the very lens
he shapes with his white spider hands
holds the answer
(though at this stage he doesn't guess)
for through it will shine the countless points of light
of the Universe itself,
a new God he will one day
apprehend and call his *causa immanens*.

Mt. Katahdin
> *"There was clearly felt the presence of a force*
> *not bound to be kind to man."*
> From *The Maine Woods* by Henry David Thoreau

Each evening a fever. The red bacillus is winning.

They have moved his little study bed down to the parlor,
and by day Sophia arranges the furniture to make fantastic shadows
on the walls for him at night:
tonight the chair becomes a mountain, the fresh-cut hyacinths are trees.

They say death is a descent, but in delirium he is climbing.

Eighty miles from Bangor by canoe
up the Penobscot,
beyond Mattawamkeag, beyond Millinocket, wearing his buttered boots
he claws his way up a steep shoulder of the mountain, grasping
at roots, stones, dead logs, the dark humus itself, slipping
on the phosphorus rot of mushrooms, finally
scrambling on all fours over the tops of flat spreading spruce trees,
their growth stunted by the cold winds,
then actually walking erect
on their branches, twelve feet off the ground.

And when at last he steps out
onto the summit,   onto huge, mist-slicked granite blocks, jumbled
as if rained from the sky, he finds a different world, far

from his ten-by-fifteen-foot cabin by the glacial pond called Walden
where he cultivated his "seven miles" of bean rows and wrote
of Nature's innocence, her balm.

This savage place is a maelstrom
of rock, water and air that sets his senses spinning like whirligigs.
He is shaking uncontrollably.
Here the heart of the matter is *matter* itself, "vast,
terrific," *matter* which contains amazing, if not dreadful, powers.

The old, terrible questions rise in his throat
to be torn from his mouth by the wind: *"Where am I? Who am I?"*

just as a monster cloud, boiling off the rocks, swallows him.

He starts up
in a paroxysm of coughing, sweat-soaked, fever
broken. Now the shadows

of the hyacinths on the wall fly back to flowers.
And the chair shadow
begins to recede slowly, like the back end of an outbound freight
train curving out from Concord into the night.

Audubon

is searching today
along the Natchez Trace, carrying
a crayon and paper, his gun, a small bottle of spirits—
the high cedars above
blue as smoke, the riverskin below brimming
with light—when
            there's a flash
of white by the marsh: a Snowy Egret,
its plumicorn
erect, still, waiting for the sense of its presence
to travel to the man before it flies.

At the tavern last night
he boasted of being the *Lost Dauphin*.
Within a year he will sit in the glittering outer parlors
of London, the *American
Woodsman,* waiting with his pictures.

Only now a simple yearning
goes out of him
and stretches toward this one shy bird in the marsh,
a longing
to hold its memory, its total
beauty, the array of its feathers in his head.
But it is not from memory he will paint it.

Later, he wires its body.
And then, as always, under the point of his brush
it becomes a languid, odd, thing,
its neck stiff, a dead

thing, not a live thing, never the vision he held
for a moment—which was

a radiance
and which died with the bird.

To A Blue-throated Hummingbird
                              (for Sheri Williamson)

Galvanic bird, gorget of blue,
you sit quietly in the palm of her hand.

Once, skins of your kind were shipped to Europe
to decorate hats,
were dried and sold in Mexico
for their magical powers.

But today you were caught alive
in the remote-controlled
drop-net
that encircles her feeder. And she has put
a tiny bracelet on your foot.

She's tall, with long brown hair
hanging in a single braid down her back, talking rapidly
to us, her students,
                about *iridescence*,
about how the granules in the feathers of your throat
are like droplets of mist in a rainbow.

She wrote the book on you.

"Blue-throats aren't like the others," she says.
"When you let them go
they like to sit in your palm for awhile."

So we all wait, staring at
your dark needle, your glittering black eyes—

for you to fly.

His Eyes

At Giverny
that perfect old-man-in-the-sky-God, Claude
Monet, portly, with a long white beard,
sits in his studio staring at his paintings of water-lilies--
then takes out a penknife and begins slashing the canvases.

He makes his way out to his garden
where he stands, silent, watching white clouds proceeding across
the blue-green expanse of his beloved lily pond.

The doctor has diagnosed cataracts.

After spending years trying to seize the unseizable light of his
exotic *nympheas:* violet, red, orange, pink, lilac, mauve and white,
now they are becoming darker and darker.

"I'm through!" he rages at the sky.

But there exists a fifth
dimension in this world, beyond space, beyond time,
called the will.

Within six months he is out again
using larger canvases, more vivid colors, trusting the labels
on his tubes of paint and looking,
looking, looking more deeply into the pond.

And something changed.

The sky, the water, the lilies
began to throb with a shifting shine, blots and slurs, smacks

of red and blue, as if the very reality of matter
was being crushed and melted down to its beginnings.

Go back and look at his last
paintings of the lily pond. Your eye drowns in an inferno of color
as you see what Claude Monet finally saw—
the trembling Universe.

The Sparks Of Creation
(for George Coffee)

Once, you stood
beneath a huge live oak tree full
of wood warblers bouncing in a sun-kindled chaos of green.

They had come far,
across the Gulf on their spring migration
to this "high island" of trees on the salt flats of south Texas.

  According to the Jewish
  mystic, Isaac Luria, God meant for
  his light to flow downward through ten holy vessels to man.

All night they had flown
through a storm, now falling out, splinters
of color, bright jewels in the trees, starved, exhausted, feeding

furiously on insects
and singing, each bird with its own name:
Yellow-throated, Blackburnian, Cerulean, Chestnut-sided.

  But a Cataclysm,
  some say creation itself, burst
  the vessels. Sparks of holiness fell into the depths.

Others too, like you,
had come, quiet people with binoculars,
to walk softly and look up at the shimmering hallucinations

in the trees, their eyes
aching, their imaginations stretched
beyond certainty in that garbled green of a dripping forest.

*The sparks were
imprisoned in the opaque shards
of the broken vessels, divine essence searching to be free.*

Once you saw them.

Sunday Morning

Ponderosa pine cathedral here
and light, with tiny
light packets sealed in sun-boiled pitch drops
smeared on gold cones.
Limelight turning
needled branches into green vitrines
as a spool-tailed breeze
scatters aspen applause above the spring
where float
dapple-drowned dead leaves.
The air piney-wine. Flicker-drum-drum,
then
silence, O the holy silence.

Good Dog

After all
a book is just a book, a poem is just a poem
and a word is just a word—
                             in the end all that matters
is
corruption of the meat.

And now death twirls his keys in his hand and whistles
for you to come.

O Savage Spirit

From Banff, from Jasper, they come
to see him. He lives in the Athabasca Glacier, a burly man

in a sheepskin coat
and rubber boots, who marches about

under the ice swinging a blue lantern. They walk up
to the toe of the glacier

and peer into his cave. They feel
his cold breath like collapsed centuries on their faces.

They walk out on the glacier and stomp
on ice a thousand feet thick and call his name.

But he never answers.
He is too busy reducing mountains to milk.

It is not
the milk of human kindness.

Bartolomé de las Casas
> *Theory of History: all overwhelming ideas*
> *begin with a nidus of pain.*

Early morning, Whitsunday, 1514,
Sancti Expiritus, Cuba...and the man they will someday call

"El Protector de los Indios" is in anguish.
He sits at a wooden table

in a thatched hut, alone, adrift in the darkness, dragging fishhooks
through his mind, reading from his diary:

"...today I witnessed another atrocity: the heads of thirty
Indians hacked off as a lesson to the rest,

what would happen to them all if they failed
to root enough gold from the earth."

A green lizard skitters up the leg of the table, after insects
drawn to his candle.

His head in his hands, he remembers that sweet smile
on the face of the most beautiful Indian girl in the village, bruised

and dead after the drunken Ortiz had finished with her,
how her legs were drawn up to fit in the small grave, how

when the first clods of dirt
struck her face, the smile came completely apart,

that torn look of death robed in terror.
Taking up the quill, he scratches: "I am convinced

that everything we have done to the Indians
thus far in the New World is unjust

and tyrannical. Because Indians have souls!"
From the white-washed church on the hill, the new bell

from Spain begins ringing. His sermon is ready.
He rises, knees stiff from sitting

all night. Razors of bright light have cut out the door.
He kicks it open.

Note To Myself

There is a silence
quiet as a church on Monday

you may call many things, but not
sun on a white wall.

You—
with the feather of faith
stuck in your throat,
mucking about, making up stories about God,

chasing lights
like a dog after a flashlight on the ground—

must accept the true flame
is a black flame,
the *Via Negativa* of Aquinas, the absence of knowing,

a silence
that is not white stones in the moonlight

Nature Trail, Saguaro National Park

                        Out here at sunset—
utter silence
and dusk, that eraser.

Old stars arriving in the blue above the sooty mountains.
Sun dumping its magma in the west.

And the tall guardians, maybe 200 years old now, bearing witness
to what?—
                        a certain stillness
beyond chattering atoms, beyond the spinning universe, beyond
even death—
                        something
only the heart can hear, the heart of sound itself.

Deep Time

can be one year
       (dinosaurs began in mid-December,
died the day after Christmas, the Roman Empire
       lasted five seconds).

It's hard to understand
            because our brains are only programmed to go
two generations back, two in front.

But we can try
       (it's giddying) to be of *two* minds—
one: a Cro-Magnon brooding beside the melting ice
                 at the center of his own day,
      and another: able
         to comprehend
that we are just a tiny bright sparkle at year's end.

Garden Of The Lost

Like some half-
remembered riff on an old hymn, drifting

into your head, the song
came to you

after a long afternoon of rainfire volleying
on the skylight of your windowless office. You were standing

on the wet black asphalt of the parking lot,
car-keys in your hand,

and had just looked up when suddenly
it slipped through a crack in a cloudbank in the west

and pierced the tiny glass ball
of a raindrop hanging from the tip of a distant pinecone,

then pierced the glass ball
of your eye.

No chorus of angels,
but a silent, visual song, a flashing needle

of light in the prismatic raindrop, going back and forth
across the spectrum,

changing color as you moved your head slightly from
side to side: blue, violet, red,

orange, yellow, green. You closed your eyes
as if to remember.

Surely this was the voice
of the old sun, breaking through. But what

was it singing? Something, something, something....
about paradise?

Judgment Day
for Tempie (1911-2001)

The bones of your clothes, the bones
of your shoes, gone.
Your craft of ash sailing into

another world, colder, lacking the purity of bones.
The will, gone
like a red thread in the wind.

Your life, a loping wolf, gone
across the fields.
Your sky torn away, the brute block of self

pulverized, scattered wide. It must be a silk
sensation, soft ash
between the fingers, or cold money

deposited in God's bank, the answer written
by gold weeds
in a slab of winter ice, a single syllable

to be plucked out with the hot, heron-toed forceps
and recited in light
of the daily burnings. By God himself. Yes or no.

Biography Note:

George Young is a retired physician living in Boulder, Colorado. He has been nominated twice for a Pushcart Prize. His first book of poems, *Spinoza's Mouse*, won the Washington Prize and was published by Word Works. He has had two chapbooks of poetry published: *Creating The Universe* by Perivale Press and more recently, *The Bird Of Paradise* by the University of Wisconsin at Madison Parallel Press. Also he has been in three anthologies of poetry by physicians: *Uncharted Lines*; *Blood & Bone*; and *Primary Care, more poems by physicians*; and in three other anthologies: *Winners, a Retrospective of the Washington Prize; Cabin Fever, Poets at Joaquin Miller's Cabin*; and *Visiting Dr. Williams*, poems inspired by the life and work of William Carlos Williams.

Reviews

Dr. Young has made a bountiful harvest of fifty-five poems, mostly in blank verse. They are sensitive and varied, about nature and about us, of large trees and tiny insects. We encounter Paul Klee, Louis Pasteur, Walt Whitman as a Civil War nurse, together with epiphanies of life and death. An inspiring collection."

- Henry Claman, MD
Distinguished Professor and Associate Director of Arts and Humanities at University of Colorado School of Medicine

George Young is a poet of nuanced perception and wide, generous feeling. Quietly and with ease he opens the universe before us and urges us to trust and to be profligate. Let yourself sway in the hammock of his lyrical voice, a voice that invites us kneel before the beauty and anguish of our scintillant world.

-Marilyn Krysl
Author of *Dinner with Osama* and *Swear the Burning Vow*

In one poem, George Young can distill the chaos and magnitude of the Big Bang down to the size and feel of a pearl in one's hand. In another, Walt Whitman is brought along on a plane ride. In yet another, Young offers "The Secret of Life." These poems concern themselves with nature, human nature, science, medicine and philosophy. They indeed offer the reader many gifts—chief among them is the author's ability to make his poems accessible while delving into a deeper realm and reaching into a higher realm. *The Astronomer's Pearl* is a remarkable collection of poetry.

-Cynthia Brackett-Vincent
Publisher/Editor, the *Aurorean*

The Astronomer's Pearl
by George Young
is the winner of the 2012
Violet Reed Haas Prize for Poetry

Previous Winners:

Penelope Scambly Schott for *The Perfect Mother*
Judge: Van K. Brock

Barbara Goldberg for *Marvelous Pursuits*
Judge: David Kirby

Seaborn Jones for *Lost Keys*
Judge: Robert Earl Price

Judith Hemschemeyer for *Certain Animals*
Judge: Judson Mitchum

Tania Rochelle for *Karaoke Funeral*
Judge: Marty Williams

Irene Willis for *At The Fortune Cafe*
Judge: Tania Rochelle

Lisa Zimmerman for *How The Garden Looks From Here*
Judge: Rick Campbell

Lana Hechtman Ayers for *Dance From Inside My Bones*
Judge: Irene Willis

Starkey Flythe for *The Futile Lesson of Glue*
Judge: John Guzlowski

Judith Hemschemeyer for *How Love Lives*
Judge: Starkey Flythe

Nagueyalti Warren for *Braided Memory*
Judge: Judith Hemschemeyer